Now we
Know about...

THE WEATHER

Dr. Mike Goldsmith

Crabtree Publishing Company
www.crabtreebooks.com

ne United States

Crabtree Publishing
616 Welland Avenue,
St. Catharines, Ontario
L2M 5V6

Crabtree Publishing
PMB 16A,
350 Fifth Avenue, Suite 3308
New York, NY 10118

Editors: Belinda Weber, Lynn Peppas, Reagan Miller
Editorial director: Kathy Middleton
Production coordinator: Kenneth Wright
Prepress technician: Kenneth Wright
Studio manager: Sara Greasley
Designer: Trudi Webb
Production controller: Ed Green
Production manager: Suzy Kelly

Picture credits:

Richard Kaylin/Getty Images: p. 19 (top)
iStock: p. 8 (bottom right), 9, 14–15, 16
National Oceanic and Atmospheric Administration: p. 14; Ralph F.
   Kresge: p. 7 (bottom)
OAR/ERL/National Severe Storms Laboratory (NSSL): p. 21 (top)
Hagg & Kropp/www.photolibrary.com: p. 15 (top)
Shutterstock: front cover, back cover, p. 1, 4–5, 8 (left), 10–11, 12–13,
   17, 18, 19 (bottom), 20, 21 (bottom), 22 (left), 23 (bottom)
Wikimedia Commons: p. 6, 7 (top), 22 (right)

Every effort has been made to trace copyright holders, and we apologize in
advance for any omissions. We would be pleased to insert the appropriate
acknowledgments in any subsequent edition of this publication.

Library and Archives Canada Cataloguing in Publication

Goldsmith, Mike, Dr.
   The weather / Mike Goldsmith.

(Now we know about)
Includes index.
ISBN 978-0-7787-4724-6 (bound).--ISBN 978-0-7787-4741-3 (pbk.)

1. Weather--Juvenile literature. I. Title.
II. Series: Now we know about (St. Catharines, Ont.)

QC981.3.G64 2009   j551.5   C2009-903116-7

Library of Congress Cataloging-in-Publication Data

Goldsmith, Mike, Dr.
  The weather / Mike Goldsmith.
     p. cm. -- (Now we know about)
  Includes index.
  ISBN 978-0-7787-4724-6 (reinforced lib. bdg. : alk. paper) --
ISBN 978-0-7787-4741-3 (pbk. : alk. paper)
  1. Weather--Juvenile literature. I. Title. II. Series.

QC981.3.G65 2009
551.5--dc22

              2009020922

Published in 2010 by Crabtree Publishing Company

Contents

What makes the weather happen? 4

What are clouds? 6

Why does the wind blow? 8

What makes it rain? 10

What makes frost? 12

What is a hailstone? 14

What is fog? 16

What happens in a thunderstorm? 18

What is extreme weather? 20

How do we know what the weather will be? 22

Glossary/Index 24

What makes the weather happen?

Weather happens because of the sun. Sunshine heats up Earth. Some places get much hotter than others. This makes the wind blow and the weather happen.

a snowstorm

Changing weather

a heavy shower of rain

The weather is always changing. It is different in places around the world. The weather changes with the **seasons**. How many different kinds of weather do you know?

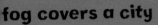 fog covers a city

What happens when Earth turns?

The Sun moves across the sky as Earth turns. It is night when your part of Earth turns away from the Sun.

Can you see the Sun every day?

Even on cloudy days, the Sun is still shining. We may not be able to see it, but it is there. Without the light from the Sun, it would be dark all the time.

When does the Sun feel hottest?

The Sun looks brighter, and feels hotter, when it is high in the sky.

What are clouds?

Most clouds are made of drops of water. The drops are so small that they float on air. Some clouds are made of ice.

What kinds of clouds are there?

There are many different types of clouds. These **cumulus** clouds look fluffy and white. These clouds are usually low in the sky.

cumulus clouds

cirrus clouds

What are cirrus clouds?

Cirrus clouds float high in the sky. They are made of tiny bits of ice.

TalKing PoinT

Can you see any clouds like the pictures on these pages?

Clouds travel across the sky quickly, so you may be able to see different types of clouds in one day.

Which clouds look flat and gray?

Stratus clouds are flat and gray. They look like blankets in the sky. Stratus clouds bring drizzle or light rain.

stratus clouds

Why does the wind blow?

The wind blows when the air is warmer in one place than another. Warm air rises. Cooler air moves in to take its place. This moving air is wind.

What is a breeze?

A slow, gentle wind is called a **breeze**. It blows dust around. A breeze makes leaves move in the trees.

What is a gale?

A **gale** is a strong, fast wind. It can break small branches off of trees. Gales can blow umbrellas inside out.

8

What is a hurricane?

Hurricanes are very strong winds that can tear down houses and trees. Hurricane winds travel at speeds of over 73 miles per hour (118 kilometers per hour).

This picture shows the damage caused to a house during a hurricane in New Orleans, Louisiana.

Talking point

Why are winds stronger on a hill than in a city?

Winds are stronger on a hill because there is a lot of open space around it. Large buildings in cities usually block the wind and keep it from blowing as strong.

WORD WIZARD!

hurricane
A very violent type of storm which causes a lot of damage

What makes it rain?

Clouds are made from tiny drops of water that float on air. When clouds get colder, the drops of water get bigger. They get too heavy to float. They fall as rain.

Raindrops look like streaks of water as they fall.

What shape is a raindrop?

Small raindrops are round. Big raindrops are shaped like jelly beans. The biggest raindrops look like tiny parachutes.

Why do we need rain?

Rain helps plants grow. It gives water for people and animals to drink. There would be no life on Earth without water.

What makes a rainbow?

You see a **rainbow** when the Sun shines through falling raindrops.

11

What makes frost?

Frost is made when the ground is freezing cold and the air is damp. When it is damp there is a lot of water in the air that we cannot see. This water turns to white ice on the ground.

What happens in very cold weather?

Ponds and lakes can freeze when it gets very cold. Rivers take longer to freeze because the water is moving. The ocean has salt water and takes even longer to freeze.

Ice collects along a beach as the ocean freezes.

We see more frost in the country than we do in cities and towns.

12

What is sleet?

Sometimes snow starts to melt as it falls to the ground. This is called **sleet**.

Sleet can make roads slippery and dangerous to drive along.

Talking point

What parts of Earth are coldest?

Antarctica is the coldest place on Earth. Only scientists live here, and they have to wear special suits to keep warm.

What is a snow drift?

Strong winds pile snow up against buildings or out in the open. These are called snow drifts.

Every snowflake is different.

What shape is a snowflake?

Snowflakes have many different shapes. Some snowflakes have six arms that look the same. Others can be thin and straight.

13

What is a hailstone?

A hailstone is a piece of ice that falls from a cloud. Many pieces fall at the same time, like rain. This is called a hailstorm.

storm clouds

What sorts of clouds make hailstones?

Hailstones are only made by storm clouds like the clouds shown above. These clouds are called cumulonimbus. They look a little bit green in color.

14

Do hailstones hurt?

Most of the time hailstones are harmless. Sometimes they are big enough to hurt people or dent cars.

Hailstones usually melt quickly once they reach the ground.

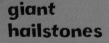

giant hailstones

Talking Point

Are hailstorms dangerous?

Hailstorms can be dangerous. Giant hailstones can dent cars and break windows. It is best to be indoors and away from windows during a hailstorm.

How big are hailstones?

Most hailstones are less than half an inch (one centimeter) across. Giant hailstones can get as big as six inches (15 centimeters) or more.

WORD WIZARD!

storm
Strong winds with rain, thunder, lightning, snow, or hail

15

What is fog?

Fog is like a cloud on the ground. It is made when the air is wet and the **temperature** gets colder. The water in the air makes small water drops that float in the air.

Why are foggy days so quiet?

It is quiet on foggy days because trucks, cars, and people move slowly and carefully.

The foggiest places are near wet areas, such as rivers, lakes, or oceans.

What is mist?

morning mist

Mist is thin fog. It is made from small drops of water in the air. Sometimes mists happen in the morning. They often happen in valleys.

mist disappears

As the day warms up, the water drops get smaller. They get so small that they cannot be seen. The mist disappears.

Talking point

Why is it often foggy near the ocean?

The air is damper near the ocean as it contains more water. In cool weather, fog collects near the coast.

WORD WIZARD!

temperature
A measure of how hot or cold something is

What happens in a thunderstorm?

Thunderstorms can bring heavy rain, **lightning**, and **thunder**. Clouds are thick and dark gray.

Most lightning is seen as jagged bolts between the clouds and the ground.

What is lightning?

Lightning is a type of electricity. Electricity is the thing that makes lights, cell phones, and televisions work.

There are about 40,000 thunderstorms across the world every day.

s lightning dangerous?

Lightning can be dangerous if it hits you. Buildings can be damaged by lightning, too. Tall buildings are protected by "lightning conductors."

Talking point

How can you tell if lightning is about to strike?

If your hair stands up during a thunderstorm, it can mean lightning is about to strike. If this happens, curl into a ball while standing on your toes. Put your hands over your ears. Never lay flat on the ground.

What is thunder?

Thunder is the sound made when lightning happens. Thunder is caused by the sudden heating of the air.

WORD WIZARD!
conductor
Something that lets electricity pass through it easily. Lightning conductors let the lightning's electricity pass straight down into the ground. It does not pass through the building.

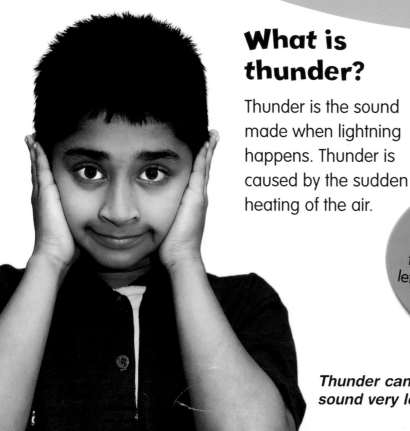

Thunder can sound very loud.

What is extreme weather?

Extreme weather is when it is very cold, very hot, very windy, or very rainy. Some parts of Earth have more extreme weather than others.

Who lives in places with extreme weather?

Not many people live in places where the weather is extreme. Most people would rather live in places where the weather is calmer.

penguins in Antarctica

Where is the weather the coldest?

The coldest weather on Earth is in Antarctica. The temperature there can fall below -112 degrees Fahrenheit (-80 degrees Celsius). That is a lot colder than inside a freezer!

What is a tornado?

A **tornado** is a tunnel of fast, spinning air. It stretches from the ground to the clouds.

A tornado touches the ground in Oklahoma.

Where is the driest place on Earth?

The driest place on Earth is in the Atacama Desert in Chile, South America. In some parts of this **desert** it has not rained for centuries.

Talking point

What makes a tornado so dangerous?

A tornado is one of nature's most powerful forces, with winds up to 298 MPH (480 km/h). Fortunately, most tornadoes are not this strong, and pass within seconds.

WORD WIZARD!
centuries
Hundreds of years

How do we know what the weather will be?

Over hundreds of years people have learned about what makes different kinds of weather. We know that on clear winter days the nights will most likely be cold and frosty. We also know that wind from the sea often brings rain.

Stevenson screen

Inside the box, scientific instruments measure changes in the air.

The instruments inside the **Stevenson screen** measure how much water is in the air. The air is damp when the weather is foggy or rainy. It is damp when wind blows from the ocean.

What is a weather forecast?

Scientists gather information about the weather. They have learned that one kind of weather follows another most of the time. They can guess what the weather might be like for the next few days. This is called a **weather forecast**.

weather chart

What will the weather be like in the future?

In the future the weather will be hotter. This is called **global warming**. Pollution can cause global warming.

Factories can cause pollution.

WORD WIZARD!
pollution
Chemicals and other things that can harm people, animals, and plants. Pollution changes the way Earth works. It can even change the weather.

Glossary

breeze Gentle wind

cirrus Feather-shaped cloud, usually white

cumulus Fluffy cloud, usually white

deserts Hot, dry land habitats

fog Cloud on the ground

frost Ice that shows up on the ground and on other things

gale Strong wind

global warming Heating of Earth

hailstone Piece of ice that falls from a cloud

lightning Flash of electricity and light from a cloud

mist Thin fog that forms near the ground

rainbow Curve of colored light in the sky

season Any of the four periods into which the year is split according to weather

sleet Snow that has started to melt

Stevenson screen A shelter for thermometers and other instruments used to measure weather conditions

stratus Flat cloud that is usually gray

temperature Measure of how hot or cold something is

thunder Sound made by lightning

tornado Huge spinning cone, made of air, which stretches from the clouds to the land or ocean

weather forecast A person's guess of what the weather will be like for the next few days

Index

B
breezes 8
C
clouds 6–7, 10, 14, 16, 18
D
deserts 21
E
Earth 5, 11, 13, 21
electricity 18, 19
F
fog 5, 16–17
frost 12

G
gales 8
global warming 23
H
hailstones 14–15
hailstorms 14–15
hurricanes 9
I
ice 6, 7, 12, 14
L
lightning 18–19
lightning conductors 19
light waves 19

M
mist 17
P
pollution 23
R
rain 4, 7, 10–11, 18
rainbows 11
S
scientists 13, 23
seasons 4
sleet 13
snow 4, 13
snowflakes 13

Stevenson screens 22
Sun 4, 5, 11
T
temperature 16, 17, 20
thunder 18–19
tornadoes 21
W
weather forecast 23
wind 4, 8–9, 13, 21, 22

Printed In the U.S.A.- CG